CUT YOUR LOSSES

CUT YOUR LOSSES

How to rebuild and grow your salon after COVID.

A helpful guide for salons and other appointment based businesses looking for a quick recovery from crisis

CAROLINE COOPER

CUT YOUR LOSSES

How to rebuild and grow your salon after COVID.

Copyright © 2020 Caroline Cooper I Profitable Salon Creator

ISBN 9798551342380

All rights reserved. No part of this book may be reproduced or distributed in any printed or electronic form without permission.

Cover and design: Caroline Cooper

*To my amazing husband, Gregory.
Thank you for all your love and support.*

TABLE OF CONTENTS

INTRODUCTION	1
PART ONE	10
CHAPTER 1 - ECONOMIC UNCERTAINTY AND THE BEAUTY INDUSTRY.	13
CHAPTER 2 - IT'S FASTER AND SAFER TO STAY IN YOUR LANE	17
CHAPTER 3 - YOUR SUCCESS STARTS WITH YOU.	22
CHAPTER 4 - MINDSET DETOX	24
CHAPTER 5 - WHERE THERE IS A WILL THERE IS A WAY	28
CHAPTER 6 - THE BEST INVESTMENT TO ENSURE YOUR SALON'S SUCCESS.	31
PART TWO	35
CHAPTER 7 – THE SHIFT TOWARDS ESSENTIALS	38
CHAPTER 8 – BUYING ONLINE	41
CHAPTER 9 – THE RISE OF PERSONALISED GOODS AND SERVICES	43
CHAPTER 10 - ARE YOU TRUSTWORTHY?	45
CHAPTER 11 - THE SHOCK TO BRAND LOYALTY	48
CHAPTER 12 - MEETING THE SHIFT IN CLIENT DEMAND	52
CHAPTER 13 - CREATING A MAGNET FOR TRIBE ATTRACTION.	56
CHAPTER 14 - AND IT'S NOT JUST CLIENTS WITH CHANGING NEEDS.	61
CHAPTER 15 - THE IMPORTANT NEW ROLE FOR SALON OWNERS.	66
PART THREE	73
CHAPTER 16 - FINDING WORKABLE SOLUTIONS.	74
QUIET OR SLOW PERIODS	
CHAPTER 17 – THE ROOT OF THE PROBLEM	77
CHAPTER 18 – KEEP THEM COMING BACK	80

CHAPTER 19 – START TALKING AGAIN	84
CHAPTER 20 – INVITE THE BEST	87
CHAPTER 21 – SHOW THEM THE WAY	89
CHAPTER 22 – MOVE THE TEAM FORWARD	93
CHAPTER 23 – GET YOUR HOUSE IN ORDER	95

HOW TO SUCESSFULLY SELL TO CLIENTS DURING DIFFICULT TIMES

CHAPTER 24 – GETTING BACK TO BASICS	99
CHAPTER 25 - KEEPING IT CONSISTENT	102
CHAPTER 26 - LET THEM KNOW THEY ARE IMPORTANT	111
CHAPTER 27 - LET THEM KNOW YOU CARE	116
CHAPTER 28 - KEEPING IT REAL	123

HOW TO STOP A STRESSFUL FEW DAYS/WEEKS/MONTHS CRIPPLING YOUR SALON CULTURE AND POSITIVITY

CHAPTER 29 – KNOW THE REACH OF YOUR CONTROL	130
CHAPTER 30 - KEEP THE COMMUNICATION FLOWING	132
CHAPTER 31 - BECOME A CREATURE OF HABIT	134
CHAPTER 32 - TRAIN LIKE YOUR LIFE DEPENDS ON IT	138
CHAPTER 33 - BRING JOY	140

THE NEXT STEPS	**146**

RESOURCES	**151**

APPENDIX 1 – WHAT A STYLIST'S REBOOKING RATES TELL YOU ABOUT THEIR SKILL AS A COMMERCIAL STYLIST.	152
APPENDIX 2 – THE 7 PARTS OF AN EFFECTIVE STYLIST PERFORMANCE PLAN	154
APPENDIX 3 – HIGH-FIVE CHART TEMPLATE	157
APPENDIX 4 – COPY OF MANTRAS FOR POSITVE SELF-BELIEF	158

ABOUT THE AUTHOR	**159**

INTRODUCTION

"They're closing all non-essential businesses and people are being asked to stay home for the next FOUR weeks. What does this all mean?" my long term client Trish exclaimed over voice message.

My thumbs stumbled as I tried frantically to find the livestream press conference on my phone, not noticing the next message arrive.

I quickly found the livestream on social media. I was bound to as it was everywhere. *"COVID-19 is here"* announced the Prime Minister.

These words brought into reality a looming threat that had been slowly rising in the community's awareness over the past 3 months.

This moment marked the point in time that would change the destiny of many small business for ever. And salons would be at the epicentre of this change.

By the time the press conference was over I had 6 more messages on my phone from Trish.

The messages were a combination of information that she had gleaned from the media, panic at the work that needed to happen in the next 48 hours before lockdown started, relief that a decision on lockdown had finally been made and an overwhelming sense of...

...what now?

Trish's collection of messages is a record of her thoughts and feelings as she lived through a moment that will stay in our collective memory for a lifetime.

I was grateful for the precious gift.

Her messages, hastily dictated as she jumped into her car to head back to her salon told me so much about her passion. Her passion for her business, her staff, her trade and the industry.

Her passion, condensed down into those quick voice messages, reflected back at me my passion for the industry. Hearing her words in that moment; vulnerable, unguarded and raw, would motivate me in the weeks and months to come.

They would motivate me to ensure that she, and other salon owners like her, had the support to not only get through this crisis but emerge confidently and profitable into the other side.

And that is the purpose of this book.

Since the start of COVID-19 I have witnessed a shift in the way we are viewing our businesses.

Our salons have always been a source of pride, an outlet for our hairdressing passions and the vehicle imagined reaching our dreams and goals in. We may have struggled at times, and been frustrated too, but success always felt within our reach. Even if we couldn't swear we knew exactly how to get there.

This crisis has caused a definite shift and change in how we view our businesses.

We are no longer so sure.

The future feels a long way off.

Success that once seemed so obtainable now feels out of reach.

So, in this book we will explore how the COVID crisis can be used to make our pathway to success even clearer.

But success feeling a long way off is not our only concern. Our lack of confidence in the strength of our business knowledge is also causing us problems.

It is leaving us paralysed with fear, anxious and unsure our businesses can absorb the cost of any mistakes.

Our salons began as a dream that would lift up our life, but is now starting to feel like a big liability that could take us and our family down with it.

We are starting to feel trapped in a vulnerable business at the mercy of forces far greater than ourselves.

It is scary.

In Section One we are going to look at how we can flip the script of fear and anxiety inducing thoughts. We look at how they stealthily creep into our minds through unguarded everyday activities and hold us captive. And then we will discover strategies to get us back on track by growing our calmness, optimism and strength.

But if dealing with feeling vulnerable was not bad enough…

…since COVID-19, we've noticed that our staff and clients are looking to us more and more for direction and reassurance.

The weight of this unspoken expectation is starting to feel crippling.

Especially, when truth be told, we do not know for sure we will get through this unscathed.

This crisis has highlighted how out of control we actually feel in our own businesses.

In Section Two we will analyse the impact of COVID on our salons and our clients and see how our role as a leader can develop to support you and your salon more effectively.

All those feelings that rushed through us in that instant the COVID-19 crisis became a reality, that moment of reckoning, have now grown and anchored within us during the months that have followed.

All the days at home, unable to effect change has left us feeling ineffective and powerless in the face of such an immense problem.

The sudden halt in revenue from being forced to close our doors has brought into light the insecure financial position we were operating in.

Leaving us feeling fraught and anxious if one client cancels or we have a few days quieter than expected.

Not knowing when this will end and how bad things could actually get highlights feelings of vulnerability and hopelessness.

And we're not the only ones.

Our staff are worried too. They look to us, but who can we turn to?

We feel alone. With no one to safely guide us through this.

We don't even have the security of knowing how long we will need to endure this economic uncertainty.

All of this has us feeling more isolated and alone as a business owner than ever before.

So in Section Three we are going to look at the practical things you can do to drive engagement, sales and profitability back into your salon post-COVID. We do this in an authentic way that is nurturing and honest and doesn't leave you feeling sleezy or salesy.

If you are feeling overwhelmed and ready for a change, you are not alone. There are other salon owners in your town, city, state, country and around the world are feeling just like you.

Although it might not feel like it right now, we are all in this together.

And if you think about it, it's really not your fault you're feeling so exposed.

Think back to when you started out in the industry as a salon junior. When you started you were trained to do that job.

As you progressed you were taught the skills that allowed you to become the hair stylist you are today.

You were taught, instructed and mentored to ensure you developed the right skills for the job in front of you.

But who has taught you to be a salon owner?

You have done it yourself. Through trial and error, through blood sweat and tears.

You have bravely taken yourself to this point, only to be handed something as awful as the COVID1-19 crisis.

It's just doesn't seem fair.

But one thing I know about salon owners is that they are champions for their businesses and will do what it takes to make their salon profitable again.

And this is what has led you here. You are looking for answers, so you have been guided to pick up this book (or downloaded it, or listen to it … you get what I mean).

In doing so you are taking a powerful step towards taking back control of your situation.

As you reading through this book you will discover there is a way out of your situation and your situation is not permanent.

You will begin to understand that this crisis which is the source of your anguish is also the provider of opportunities to grow your business beyond your wildest dreams.

Your confidence will grow as you realise there are solutions to problems that seem unmovable, and that all the problems in your business are overcomeable (is that even a word?)

You will have understood that there is a magic key to creating a salon that is robust enough to not only get through this, but to thrive.

And that key is you.

Even if you don't feel it right now, by the end of the book you will recognise that you have what it takes to be the change you and your salon need.

After reading this book you will know how to focus your energy on the things that really shift the needle in your business and move your salon and your team forward.

You will understand the importance of directing your passions towards developing how you operate as a salon leader.

In turn, you will see that your new leadership strength will create a real pathway for your staff to be able to support your salon to become thriving and profitable, even in these crisis moments.
And most importantly, you will have a plan to start taking your first steps towards recovery, and beyond.

By reading this book you have given yourself the peace-of-mind and calmness we all need, at this time, to thrive.

PART ONE

Taming the beast of uncertainty

Our salons' success is a direct measure of our mental resilience and hard work.

Successful salons are not forged in the sands we are known to bury our heads in when the going gets tough.

They are forged through overcoming the sizeable challenges put in front of us and our determination to not just meet them, but to overcome them.

If our salons are to stand any chance of getting through the COVID crisis they are going to need us to be fighting fit and have a champion's attitude.

In this section we will uncover:

- Why we should be optimistic. There are opportunities as well as problems in times of crisis.

- Where to find the information that successfully solves our problems without overwhelming us.

- How to keep calm in the face of constant bad news.

- How to detox our mind and keep it battle ready to face each day.

- And how to trust in ourselves and believe that we do have what it takes to be our salon's hero.

CHAPTER 1 - ECONOMIC UNCERTAINTY AND THE BEAUTY INDUSTRY.

"These are unprecedented times." We hear it over and over again from well-meaning government officials who are trying to keep us informed.

This comment is vague and anxiety inducing for any business owner or employee.

Even more worryingly, we have to ask ourselves, "If the officials don't know what to expect, how can I?"

The short answer is we don't.

Certainly not when it comes to how long or how hard the impact of COVID-19 will be on our businesses.

But there are some things we do know, and most of these should be a source of hope for salon owners.

When we look at what is happening, we need keep some perspective.

The first thing to remember is that salons have been through periods of economic upheaval before.

And survived.

One of the key supporting reasons for this, is that in times of economic downturn or uncertainty, people don't stop spending; rather they change the way in which they do it.

What history tells us is that when people start to feel the pull of the tides of economic change they adapt the way they spend.

The first things to go are the big ticket items. The overseas holidays, weekends away, a new car, new TV or new laptop are off the list.

Then the next thing they do, is treat themselves so they don't feel like they are missing out.

Evidence shows that as spending on consumer goods falls, we see a correlating rise in spending on feel-good products and services.

These include things likes meals out and take-aways, alcohol, streaming subscriptions, clothes, chocolates and….

      …hair and make-up products and services.

Finally, some good news.

This point highlights one of the hidden secrets of economic downturns, and that is: The money doesn't go away, it is just in a different place.

Even though it may feel like it's no longer there or that it's harder for us to earn, the truth is we just need to approach the problem of finding the money differently.

We're trying to earn money as we did pre-COVID-19.

The pre-COVID-19 ways are drying up

BUT...

...the post-COVID-19 ways are still untapped.

Once we understand this, it opens our eyes up to all the new opportunities available to us now, that weren't there at the beginning of 2020.

We've all heard experts talking about pivoting in business. It's a new buzz word being used in terms like, "Pivoting through crisis" and "Pivoting into success".

They are talking about discovering the new opportunities to earn money that are here now for us to access.

This is what they are talking about.

Even when everything looks bleak there is a beacon of light leading us back to profitability.

It is important to hold this in mind as we move through this book and discover the mindset and business practices that will allow you to grab hold of these hidden opportunities and run with them in your salon.

CHAPTER 2 - IT'S FASTER AND SAFER TO STAY IN YOUR LANE

I could feel my heart start to race as I scrolled through the newsfeed on my Social Media.

My thumb was quickly flicking past images of pain, poverty and crisis mixed between photos of people who were living their best lives in full Social Media glory, ads, and pictures of government officials with serious faces and even more serious warnings about what was to come.

I could feel the panic rising.

Would we get through? Is there enough money saved? Do I have enough? Why do I feel like I am the only one struggling through this? What's wrong with me?

I could hear the chatter of pessimism growing in my head as my mind, egged on by the relentless steam of images in my hand, grew louder and more frantic.

Then I looked up.

What greeted my eyes was in stark contrast to the feelings of doom I was now feeling.

The sun was shining down on a bustling car park filled with enthusiastic Saturday morning shoppers.

A couple hurried past me. Hands clasping re-usable shopping bags brimming with fresh produce, while deep in conversation about what to serve their friends that night at a dinner they were hosting.

Their words slightly muffled by the COVID masks they now wore, but they were animated and enthusiastic. Visually joyful at their plans for the future.

In this reality, life was good. It was positive.

What I had been seeing on social media was a collection of opinions others were sharing about their reality, and it had sucked me in and left me traumatised.

But the feelings and thoughts I was having about the world after focusing so intently on my phone did not match my physical reality.

In that moment I realised that I was robbing myself of this reality, by living through the opinions others hold about their situation.

This is a lesson we all need to hear.

When it comes to finding out about what is going on in the world, be mindful of who and where you get information from.

We all know how tempting it is to be scandalised by the mess others have made and the drama in their lives.

Heck, that is how the media sells to us and captures so much of our attention.

The media is expert at framing things in attention grabbing ways that can feel quite shocking, so it can be hard for us to know exactly how things really stand.

We need to be gentle on ourselves. We don't need to try and understand everything that is going on in the world.

When it comes to keeping positive, this is not helpful.

So we just need to be mindful that there is a lot of hype out there.

Be mindful of hype and look, for a more balanced approach.

When it comes to creating a more positive mindset, we need to be careful of who's opinion we take on board.

Just because it sounds important or interesting, doesn't mean it's important to *our* journey.

Everyone's opinion comes from their experience and beliefs about the world. It's important to remember that an opinion is not necessarily helpful information, even if it feels like it at the time.

Align yourself with those who have a world view closer to the one you want for yourself.

Just as a negative world view can increase our anxiety, a positive world view can bring calm.

To stay positive and armed with the most useful information and news for us, there is one trick I'm going to share with you.

Keep your focus local.

Is that it?

Quite simply, yes.

We need to retrain our minds to sharpen our focus onto *our reality* as well as we have been conditioned to with social media.

Check in regularly and mindfully with the things around you that actually matter to you and effect your life and well-being.

Checking in with valuable things like our family, our community, our salon, our clients and our staff will mean we can gather information that is actually useful to us.

The information we collect from checking in locally is the information that will really help us move forward.

The truth is, what we discover when we put down our phones and check in with our real life worlds may not always be easy to hear.

We may feel the information more deeply but, it will always be helpful and doing something with that information is something we can control.

Knowing what is within our control, and letting it go when it is not, is the route to creating a calmer and more focused future.

We all need that right now.

CHAPTER 3 - YOUR SUCCESS STARTS WITH YOU.

I am a fan of Medieval History. I'm not going to bore you with details or stories from the past, rather, I am going to impart to you something that I have noticed from reading history.

There has never been an army that has won a battle, easily or against all odds, that didn't have a strong leader at the helm.

And the stronger the leader, the more powerful the army and the more that it can conquer.

You may be wondering, "How does this relate to getting my salon out of this COVID hole?"

It's a metaphor that tells us that to increase your chances of winning against COVID your salon needs a strong leader.

And the stronger the leader you can find, the more the salon can achieve.

So where do you find a strong leader?

I feel like I don't even need to answer this because deep down we all already know that we find it in *ourselves*.

We may not feel like strong leaders right now, and that's OK.

This is the part of the book where we discover what we can do to arm ourselves properly to be the strongest leader we can.

As you read through Part 1 you may find you already know a lot of this information, if that is the case then just take it as recognition you are already on the right track to reaching your leadership potential.

If this is new information, take your time. It's important for developing in your role as a leader that you cultivate a mindset that has the strength and resilience to move you and your salon forward.

CHAPTER 4 - MINDSET DETOX

The biggest challenge everyone faces when it comes to being a strong leader in their own lives is their insecurities.

As humans we have a bad habit of getting in our own way too often and second guessing our own skills and potential. Stopping us from reaching our potential as leaders and business owners.

We are all guilty of listening to that pesky voice inside our head that reminds us we're not good enough, the consequences will be too great, that we don't deserve this, that everything that could go wrong will go wrong.

And when our world is starting to spin out of control it is really tempting to join the pity party of excuses and give ourselves permission to not do what needs to happen.

So how do we quieten that voice of discontent to allow us to take action confidently?

By slowing down and finding release from anxiety.

It's about getting back to basics and working on a positive and resilient mindset through ramping up our mental health routine.

There are many ways you can do this. I do not rank any one tool over the others, and this is not a definitive list by any stretch of the imagination.

Take from the list what you want and leave what doesn't serve.

The key thing here is that we take the action needed to honour our place as our businesses' leaders and support ourselves to fulfil this role to the best of our ability by taking care of our mental health.

Things that help put us in a positive mindset:

- Meditation
- Practicing Gratitude and Thankfulness for what is working
- Mindful actions (doing things deliberately and with purpose. No multi-tasking here.)
- Yoga
- Running, hiking or walking
- Spending time in nature
- Walking barefoot
- Playing sport
- Swimming
- Cleaning and removing clutter from our spaces
- Increasing the amount of fresh fruits and vegetables in our diet
- Spending engaged time with loved ones (play a board game, read together, listen to each other, laugh together)

- Reading or doing a craft. Practice your non-digital skills like knitting, carpentry, cake decoration, embroidery, even adult colouring books.
- Singing
- Dancing
- Learning a new skill. It could be juggling, archery, or how to play a musical instrument.
- Planning your goals
- Writing a list. It could be a bucket-list, vacation ideas, a description of your ideal partner, things to be thankful for, or what you'll do different next time around.
- Calling a friend for a chin-wag
- Going to a therapist
- Taking a trip away

Things that we may think help but actually don't:

- Partying
- Drinking
- Drugs
- Late nights or irregular bedtimes
- Too much coffee or sugar
- Sitting for too long
- Watching TV
- Spending too much time on our device

- Listening to the radio (not just music)
- Not saying NO enough
- Not asking for help
- Putting unrealistic expectations on our ourselves.

It's important that we take our time and try things we can sustain as part of our routine.

If we find ourselves doing activities that we know need to change, it's important we are gentle on ourselves and give ourselves the space to let go of those less positive coping strategies we have picked up over time.

We should be looking for consistent effort toward positive choices.

This is the most sustainable way ahead.

CHAPTER 5 - WHERE THERE IS A WILL THERE IS A WAY

Self-belief is so important for success in business, but it can be so hard to find.

Knowing that you are capable and are willing to do what it takes to make the changes, no matter how scary they may appear, is critical in shaping your success as a salon leader.

Self-belief is developed in childhood through the establishment of positive and supportive relationship founded in unconditional love.

But some of us were not lucky enough to have this cultivated in us during childhood.

For others our confidence has been rocked by a number of unfortunate relationships or events during our adulthood that has eroded, or completely wiped out, any self-belief.

What then? How do we get self-belief if we have lost it, or never had it in the first place?

> Again, the answer is found in us.

It is about creating a positive and supportive relationship with ourselves first, founded in unconditional love.

"Well that sounds simple enough." I can almost see you rolling your eyes.

You're right, it's not.

But there is one simple thing we can do that can really shift our self-belief quickly.

And that is telling ourselves positive mantras.

The following are some mantras that are helpful in quickly shifting how we feel about ourselves and our role as a leader in our salon.

I encourage you to write these out and stick them to your bathroom mirror and recite them to yourself every day.

The more regularly you do this, the quicker you will see results.

Mantras for cultivating positive self-belief and leadership success:

I am worthy

I am doing the work needed

I am not alone

Others are excited by my success

I am working every day to get through this

I am investing in my personal growth

My personal growth is important

I am a strong leader in my salon

I ask for help when I need it

Success is on its way to me

My team is energised by my leadership

My salon thrives under my leadership

Abundance flows from the work I do as a leader

CHAPTER 6 - THE BEST INVESTMENT TO ENSURE YOUR SALON'S SUCCESS.

OK, so I want to let you in on a little secret.

A BIG secret actually.

This is that one secret bit of information I think you may have been looking for.

This is the secret that will transform your salon so you can get through, not only COVID, but anything the future throws at you.

It is the secret every salon owner who has a thriving business that truly supports their goals and dreams knows.

It is a secret known by every successful person that has ever existed.

There is not ONE successful person in the world who doesn't know this secret.

If you don't believe me, you can test it.

Once you know it, ask any successful person and they will confirm that in knowing this secret you are now on the route to success.
And I am going to let you in on it.

And the BEST news is...

...just by picking up this book, you have started to unlock the secret's power.

SO here it is...

If you want to achieve success, not just in business but in every area of your life you need to invest ...

... in ...

... YOU!

That's it.

Investing in you is the best investment you could ever make in your business.

Spending time and energy growing your knowledge and understanding of what makes a good salon good, and then a great salon great, is critical if we want our salons to become good and grow into great.
As an industry, we are comfortable at investing in technical skills training.

But so reluctant to spend our precious time and hard earned money on learning how to run our businesses properly.

And I get it.

We have been running our salons this long, we should know everything important there is to know ... right?

We understand hairdressing but business management sounds like stuff we should outsource to professional sounding people like Accountants and Administrator ... isn't it?

We might find other people will judge us if they think we need help learning how to run our salon ... do you think?

The truth is investing in yourself is critical for your success.

It is the ONLY path to success.

And the exciting news is you've taken a step down that path my buying this book and reading it (or listening to it).

Success is hard to find without the commitment and sacrifice of time, money and, most importantly, effort.

But the good news is that this investment pays dividends.

Whatever we spend on developing ourselves and our knowledge, we get back again and again, and in ways we can't even imagine right now.

As we move through the rest of this book we will learn and grow our knowledge of how to get our salons through this COVID crisis in the best shape.

We will discover the opportunities the COVID crisis has created.

We will find out what your clients and staff need you to be doing to support them.

We will uncover where your focus as the owner now needs to be.

And we will work through strategies to tackles the problems COVID has revealed in our salons, allowing us to develop a plan to move forward towards success.

Let's go.

PART TWO

The New Normal

When a client sits down in our chair, before we get to work transforming their hair, we need to know some information.

We need to know what we are working with so we ask questions about their history and do a hair and scalp analysis.

Then we need to find out what they want from us so we can create a hairstyle that will excite them and keep them coming back.

So too it is with the COVID crisis.

First, we have to look at where we are now and analyse what has changed since the start of COVID.

Then we need to find out what our staff and clients want from us so we can create a salon that excites them and keeps them coming back.

Finally, we will look at how our responsibility as a salon owner has changed, and why we all need to rethink our business priorities.

Things have changed since COVID.

That much is obvious but what is less obvious is how this impacts upon our salons and appointment based businesses.

As we work through this part of the book we will look at the impact COVID-19 has had, and continues to have, on our markets.

The information presented to you probably won't come as a revelation, rather a gentle focussing of your awareness.

You will probably find you know exactly what I am talking about as soon as you read it.

Sometimes it's just about information being highlighted to you, rather than learning it.

CHAPTER 7 – THE SHIFT TOWARDS ESSENTIALS

Consumer trends are changing, and fast. Keeping up with the changes can be daunting.

Here we look at the emerging trends and investigate how they relate to the salon.

To begin with, as physical freedoms and incomes have reduced, consumers are making a sudden and dramatic shift towards purchasing more essential items and away from things they view as luxury or non-essential.

The nature of a lockdown situation means that often consumers have been unable to access non-essential items even if they wanted to.

And even in regions that have experienced lower levels of lockdown restrictions this trend has also been followed as people finding the effects of COVID impacting on their regular routines and personal finances.

And as previous economic downturns have taught us, as personal budgets tighten and general optimism about economic recovery dips, so too does spending on luxury goods and big-ticket items.

But as anyone who has spent any time in lockdown will tell you, hairdressers feel like an essential service.

This is good news for salon owners.

Although our salons may feel quieter, people are still willing to brave the pandemic to come and see us to get their hair done.

People are also still buying personal products like shampoo and conditioner. These are, after all, essential items.

There is some movement towards people choosing lower priced alternatives for these items, but the important thing to note is that they are still buying them.

When we are recommending our products to clients there should be a real focus on the value of the product that may not be obvious from the price alone.

So even if the salon product is more expensive, clients should be encouraged to view it as better value for money due to the added benefits for the client's hair.

Value such as the little amount of product required and therefore the amount of uses from one bottle, the enhanced results and quality of care for the hair and scalp the product offers are all things that can help clients to view salon products as essential and value for money.

It will be important for salons moving forward to be aware of the essential element of clients having their hair done. Reminding and reinforcing this with the language we use and emphasis placed on this in communicating with clients will help ensure clients keep coming back.

CHAPTER 8 – BUYING ONLINE

As consumers are less and less able to access physical shops they are increasing their demand on online shopping. And looking at the steady stream of courier vans hitting our streets, this trend looks like it is here to stay.

As consumers who may not traditionally purchased online have become more and more reliant on it, they have also had more and more positive experiences with it.

The ease of being able to browse and compare products in the comfort of their own homes at a time that suits them means that more and more consumers a making online shopping their preferred means of spending.

Salons are service based businesses so rely on consumers coming into the store, so how can this trend be leveraged in our salons?

It's important that we have an online presence. This goes beyond just a Social Media page or pages.

Consumers are wanting to check us out online before they visit.

They want to know where we are, what our salon looks like. What work our salon produces and what products we use.

They want to know what our salon stands for and how this aligns with their personal values.

They also want to book online. Consumers are less and less likely to approach a new salon by calling them. Online booking allows consumers to feel they have more control over their relationship with the salon by giving them the ability to manage their own appointment.

And consumers are looking to buy products online.

My clients who have added online shops to their websites have noticed a whole new market opening up to them.

Clients who will never come to them because they live too far away are now purchasing loyally from their online store.

And on the flip side. The reason salons with online purchasing are growing the market for their products is because salons are not offering and selling these products to their clients authentically.

If we don't talk about the products we are using on our clients and not offering them properly and regularly to our clients we can be sure our clients are taking notes and looking for them online to purchase from someone else.

CHAPTER 9 – THE RISE OF PERSONALISED GOODS AND SERVICES

The increase in demand for personalised goods and services is a trend that has been on the rise for at least the last 5 years but has been given a massive shot in the arm by COVID.

As people live more and more of their everyday lives online there can be a tendency to feel lost in a crowd.

Posts go uncommented on, likes just aren't what they used to be and personal comments go unnoticed.

The mass of noise that is the internet has given rise to a cult of individualism.

People want to feel both special and connected.

This need for acknowledgement as a special individual has seen a rise in demand for personalised products online.

There are online hair care producers that compete with our salon products that give consumers the ability to personalise everything from the colour, fragrance, purpose and even the name on the bottle.

Now that is a tough act to follow.

But us salons, we have been personalising for ever. That is our thing.

And now is the time to remind clients about it by making more conscious choices in the language we use when recommending to our clients.

It is about communicating with our clients when we are personalising their cut or colour.

Ask them if they would like a personalised treatment, tailored to address their concerns with their hair, added to their service.

Show them your professionally personalised regime of products for them to take home to ensure all their hair needs are taken care of.

Personalisation increases consumer interest and buy-in.

CHAPTER 10 - ARE YOU TRUSTWORTHY?

In an age of contrasting opinions and radically changing circumstances it can be hard for consumers to know who to trust.

Consumers nowadays know about filters, wigs, lighting and photoshopping.

They understand that content can be crafted to project a more favourable picture than reality.

Even if we have a great online presence, that includes beautiful and genuine before and after shots, how do consumers know that spending their hard-earned money with us will leave them satisfied?

How can they be sure we are as good as we say we are?

The answer is reviews.

Reviews are a current client's honest and genuine feelings about how your salon left them feeling.

They reliably let future or returning clients know what they can expect.

There are many places you can collect reviews.

You can do in online with public platforms like Google Reviews or Facebook.

Through your website you can encourage clients to send you feedback and then choose the best for your marketing material.

You can encourage clients to leave a written review or feedback as part to an in-salon promotion.

Or directly canvas clients with a survey using your mailing list. Google Forms or Survey Monkey are two cheap and easy to use options, but there are many more available online.

But how do you get clients to leave reviews?

The simple answer is …

… ask.

If you think you did a 5-star service, ask them to leave a 5-star review on your preferred platform.

Asking for reviews is a great incentive to run with your staff. Encouraging your stylists to ask their clients for reviews and then rewarding them for every ten 5-star reviews they get.

This is a powerful way to both grow your salon's reviews while keeping stylists focused on their performance.

CHAPTER 11 - THE SHOCK TO BRAND LOYALTY

Since COVID, getting our preferred consumer brands when we want them has become increasingly difficult.

COVID has created problems with supply for some brands, especially for those manufactured in regions that have experienced long or tough lockdowns, or those that require components from multiple regions to manufacture.

We have also noticed it when it comes to booking appointments for the hairdresser after coming out of lockdown periods.

And with so many people now working from home, finding time to go to their regular hairdresser, that may be located nearer their workplace than home, can become an issue leaving them looking for someone new and available nearby.

The changing circumstances around the supply of product and the availability of appointments has become an issue.

The impact is that consumers are trying new brands.

And they are doing in it in larger numbers than ever before.

For salons, this means the security of our hard-won client base is under threat.

But it also means there are more clients out there who are prepared to try new brands.

The trick here is to retain our current clients _and_ draw these potential new clients towards us at the same time.

Easier said than done though, isn't it?

Well you might find it is a lot easier than you think.

In this chapter we will look at how to retain the clients we do have, and in the next few chapter we will explore things new clients are now looking for in a salon so we can attract more of those clients that are on the move.

When it comes to retaining our current clients, there is one thing that should be our top focus.

> That one thing is our rebooking rate.

And I cannot emphasise enough the importance of maintaining a high rebooking rate.

Rebooking does two things for us.

Firstly, it locks in the client and greatly improves the chance of them coming back.

The availability of future appointments where and when they want them is the biggest motivator at this time for clients to try somewhere else.

By locking in a future appointment by rebooking before leaving the salon, clients feel more secure, and we can relax knowing that future work (and income) is scheduled.

To improve rebooking rates in our salons it is important that we are actively working with our stylists to train and monitor their rebooking.

Due to the unsettling nature of COVID, clients are less future focused so they can be more reluctant to commit to future plans that they may have to changed later.

Developing a clear rebooking policy and procedure that doesn't penalise the client for making last minute changes due to COVID, and training our stylists to deliver it successfully, will give our stylists the tools to grow our clients' confidence that their place within the salon is secure and supported.

And this brings me on to the second benefit of rebooking.

It gives us permission to contact the client directly.

If a client has a future appointment booked in, it is reasonable to call them about that appointment if we need to.

If our salon is shut for a lockdown period or one of our staff needs to be off work suddenly, we have permission to call the client to change or reschedule the appointment to better support your salon workflow management.

If we don't have clients rebooked we have to sit there and wait to see if clients call to know how our day will pan out.

Without rebooked clients we have to wait until clients are ready to prioritise contacting us about an appointment to get their hair done.

Rebooking clients reduces our feelings of vulnerability by increasing our control over appointments.

CHAPTER 12 - MEETING THE SHIFT IN CLIENT DEMAND

In the last chapter we looked at how growing our salon's rebooking rate is key to retaining the clients our salon currently serve.

So in the next couple of chapters we will explore what else is going on in the markets since COVID and what this means for salons when it comes to attracting new clients and how to share our brand in a way that speaks to our market.

COVID and the events of 2020 have thrown life as we know it up in the air, given it a good old shake, and sent it tumbling back down to earth for us to pick up the pieces.

This has left us all questioning things about ourselves.

It is forcing us to re-evaluate who we are, what we stand for and, most importantly, where do we fit in to the new post-COVID world?

People are now looking for their authentic tribe that fits their new and improved self-awareness.

Clients now want to know:

    Who are the brands that serve people like them?

Who gets them?

Which brands stand for the same things they do?

The more salons communicate with potential clients about these things, the more we attract the clients aligned with our brand ...

... and in greater numbers too.

Salons attract and gather the right clients by demonstrating how we understand them and how the ways we offer services and products works for them.

Clients need to feel like they belong. They need to feel they belong to a tribe that gets them and understands their unique situation in a rapidly changing world.

A world in which clients are increasingly aware of personal safety but have their own definition of what that should mean.

Feeling physically vulnerable from poor or inadequate health and safety practices is the number one anxiety clients face when it comes to getting back in the chair.

Having clear, well-practiced and consistent health and safety procedures will reassure nervous clients and bring comfort to clients that are looking for the standard of care you offer.

And it's not just physical health that clients are paying attention to.

They are also looking at how well we support and care for each other.

They are looking at how we treat our staff, support our community and get behind the causes that matter to them.

They also want to know we understand that their routines have changed.

They are looking to know how our salons can support them in the new 'Homebody Economy'.

The Homebody Economy is a term that was created to capture the driving forces behind economic decisions consumers are making because they are staying home more.

Staying home more is affecting how consumers need businesses to operate.

In an economy where the 9-to-5 grind is no longer a thing, they what to know what hours we are available for them.

As clients are working from the kitchen table and home-schooling the kids during the week, clients want to know what days over the weekend we are open. They want to know which days we are working late, or maybe early.

Clients want to know what new ideas you offer in our salons to support their need to physically distance from people.

Do we share information with them online on how they can change up their style at home?

Can they order the products they see us use in our social media online and have them delivered?

Do we offer 'Netflix and Chill' pamper packs that they can purchase as a treat for themselves to do at home as a fabulous boredom buster?

We need to get creative and step into our client's shoes. We need to ask what has changed for them physically, emotionally and with their lifestyle?

What can we do differently or offer in a new way to attract our tribe to our salon brand?

CHAPTER 13 - CREATING A MAGNET FOR TRIBE ATTRACTION.

When it comes to attracting our tribe to us there is only one way to do this successfully ...

... and that is with *authentic communication*.

Authentic communication comes from the heart. From the heart of the salon. And is true to how the salon operates.

To communicate authentically we need to understand what we have to say to our market that will allow them to understand who we are, so they will know if they should come to us.

This is not about creating binge-worthy content or pushing every offer and idea.

It is about revealing the essence of our salon, what we stand for, and how we do things every time we communicate with our clients and our market.

The following are some simple (but not necessarily easy) steps to creating authentic communication that attracts the right people towards you.

1. **Understand what your salon has to offer and share that message in everything you say and do.**

   To discover what it is your salon has to offer think about how you would answer the following questions.

   a. *Where you are heading?* This is basically the reason your salon exists in the market. How would you describe your salon's purpose? What do you want your salon to be known for? (Even if you're not there yet?)

   b. *Why this is important?* Why do people need to know about what you do?

   c. *How are you going to get there?* How do you do things? What values do you live by and support?

   d. *What is the impact you hope to make on the way?* How will your salon's journey improve the lives of others?

   Now, the answers you have to these questions don't necessarily need to be ground-breaking or revolutionary.

   But they can be.

   The key here is; they have to be authentic.

2. **Develop truth in your message.** How believable is what we are saying? Think about the ways we are communicating with our market. Are the messages consistent?

The following are some places where we send strong messages to our market, but we might not even be aware we are doing so.

a. When people look at your Social Media, do your posts support your salon's message, or merely promote something?

b. When clients and potential clients come into your salon, how aligned are your staff with your message? Is there evidence of training, processes and structure to guide staff to live your salon's story every day?

c. How does your customer service, and even the hairdressing services you offer, match your salon's message? Are all stylists living your salon's message with every client, everyday?

Communication with our clients happens in more ways that just through posts and carefully crafted email messages.

It happens at every touch point with our clients.

It is in the care taken to look after the salon, the leadership behind the team, and planning and training that goes into the service delivery.

It is important to ensure that our salon's message is consistent through all these places.

3. **Communicate openly with love and kindness.** Authentic communication is natural and it is a two-way process.

    When we communicate with our market, we need to be aware about the ways our market can communicate back to us.

    It is also important that we are open and receptive to this communication from our market.

    Even when the communication back feels like criticism, it is actually just genuine feedback. It is an opportunity to learn how to do things better.

    One of the most powerful ways to get communication back from your clients is through your staff.

    Our stylists work one-on-one with our clients daily and are powerful channel for communication between our market and us.

    Nurturing the lines of communication is important.

    Creating strong systems that have multiple opportunities of staff to safely and authentically communicate with you as part of their usual routine will support this.

Strong systems create routine and structure.

Routine and structure creates a powerful foundation for trust.

Trust happens when Stylists know they have safe platforms for sharing, that their voices are listened to, and most importantly, they can trust our reaction, as the salon owner, to feedback.

CHAPTER 14 - AND IT'S NOT JUST CLIENTS WITH CHANGING NEEDS.

COVID has also brought about changes for our staff too.

Stylists are feeling more vulnerable.

They have increased concerns for their physical safety.

Their emotional burden from clients has increased, creating pressure on their mental health.

They are worried about their jobs.

They are really becoming increasingly aware of how vulnerable they are financially.

Despite all this, stylists still want to do a good job.

But their growing insecurities can hold them back from working how we need them to.

When we look at the struggles our staff are facing at the moment, they can be split into two broad categories.

1. Reduced financial freedom

2. Increased stress

Let's start with reduced financial freedom and see how this impacts on their work. What does reduced financial freedom mean?

It means that stylists are more aware of their financial position.

They may wonder if their job is safe.

They may wonder whether they have enough money to get through the coming months.

In a nut-shell, money, or rather a lack of it, is at the forefront of the stylists minds.

And it is easy for stylists to project this mindset onto their clients.

They make the assumption that their clients can no longer afford what they are offering, so they don't offer.

They care about their clients and don't want to upset them by suggesting a service they may not be able to afford, so they don't fully advise the client.

They believe that their clients no longer have the budget for products they have been purchasing, so they don't recommend or remind clients about take-home products.

When the truth is that the stylist does not actually know what their clients can or cannot afford.

A stylist's fears about the scarcity of money stops them giving clients the service they have come in for.

But a belief that clients can't spend money is not the only insecurity that stops them offering and recommending to their clients.

Increased stress on the stylist means they want a calm environment.

The best way for stylists to manage this themselves is by not imposing themselves on their clients.

When stylists feel stressed they withdraw and they are less likely to offer products, recommend services or give advice.

This means stylists stop selling.

If they're not offering, then they can't be told NO.

If they're not told no, then in their mind, the client must be happy with them.

But this is rarely the case.

Clients want the full service, they want full value from their salon experience, especially when money is tight.

They also want the respect to make purchasing decisions for themselves and not have assumptions made about them.

When stylists are left on their own to work guided by these insecurities, stylists are in effect, denying clients the value of the service they came into the salon for.

This will lead to unhappy clients and reduced revenue.

It is important that we have systems in our salons to support and guide stylists through stressful times.

Without them, we are in effect, allowing our stylists' insecurities to dictate the level of our salon's performance.

When your salon has strong systems for performance standards, offers regular training and links service outcomes to wages and opportunities for promotion, it is a great way to ensure stylists continue to work to our standards, keeping our clients happy and our profits healthy. Strong systems help our stylists leave their insecurities at the door.

CHAPTER 15 - THE IMPORTANT NEW ROLE FOR SALON OWNERS.

COVID has thrown a lot of changes our way. And there is one change that has come steaming towards us as salon owners that we can't avoid.

This is the need for a sudden and dramatic re-evaluation of our role within our businesses.

Whether we like it or not, salon owners are now finding ourselves having to step up front and centre in our salons with authentic and regular communication and strong leadership for our team and our clients.

This is the sign that is signalling very strongly that change is afoot.

COVID is demonstrating that salon owners are needing to move more regularly and more purposefully into the space of salon management and salon CEO.

SALON OWNERSHIP

Artist → *Management* → *CEO*

There will be some salon owners who want to stay in the space of artist and stylist.

COVID has provided us with that opportunity to reflect and evaluate what's going to be best for us as individuals moving forward.

As a result, some salon owners will be making a conscious decision that the most important aspect of being a salon owner is being able to be a strong stylist and artist.

This is where they find their flow.

This is what's important to them.

So the industry will see some owners making a conscious decision to change the way they operate.

They will look to step away from the ownership space, and move into being independent stylists or going back to work for other people in salons, where they can be supported to flourish in the space they choose for themselves.

And this is totally okay.

It is a personal choice and a personal journey.

But for most owners, they will want to develop their ownership role, recognising a growing need to manage their teams and grow their salon's profits and to consistently deliver these profits.

If we want to continue our journey as salon owners, and get our salons through this crisis, we will need to actively step away from the role of stylist and into the roles of salon manager and salon CEO more regularly.

In the role of salon manager, our main role will be growing our stylists so they can grow their revenue, which in turn will grow our salon's profits.

When we're in the space of CEO, we will be spending more time planning, strategizing and creating new and novel ways to grow our businesses and our wealth.

So our two new priorities as a salon owner need to be:

> *Managing our team to grow our profits and ...*

> *... strategizing how to use these profits to grow our wealth.*

Growing your profits and growing your wealth should now be your number one priorities as a salon owner, and let me tell you why.

As salon owners we are naturally nurturing and humble people so it can feel a little jarring against our personal values to be unapologetic about growing your profits and your wealth.

But if COVID has told us anything, it is that this is now our job.

And there is an important reason for this.

Improving salon profits gives both the salon and the stylists who work in it increased opportunities to thrive.

Increased profits provides money for training and resources to adapt to changes quickly, more access to opportunities for new revenue streams and the ability to offer real support when it is needed.

It is hard to be adaptive when there is nothing to financially support change and growth.

Increased profits also support wealth creation, which is the other part of our new priority as a salon owners.

When we focus on growing our wealth, we can proudly say we are protecting our businesses and the people who work for them.

Growing wealth means two things:

1. Paying down debt, so we owe less money
2. Growing our equity, so we own more outright.

But why are these things important?

Because anyone who has been in business for any period of time will know, economic storms will return again and again.

It's the nature of being in business.

Economic pressure will come in different shapes and different magnitudes throughout our business careers.

COVID is just the latest, really bad, one ...
... but it won't be the last.

And it is our wealth that protects us against these storms.

When we have some wealth, we have something to leverage against.

It's easier to find financial lifelines if we don't have piles of credit card debt and multiple mortgages on our home.

And being able to get these resources not only supports our business, but the women who work in them too.

Creating financial flexibility allows us to more easily jump through the obstacles that come with operating in a modern economic environment.

Having financial reserves means that when things like COVID happen, we can still pay our tax bill, that we can still pay our staff, that we can still pay our landlord.

So why do we need to be unapologetic about this and spend more of our time in this space, proudly focusing on profitability and growing wealth?

It is simply that being financially prepared reduces our stress.

Having been proactive in creating a financial safety net, by developing our leadership skills and salon systems to support our stylists to grow their revenue means that we can approach crisis with a calmer and more resilient mindset.

When we have created that ability to be able to pivot, move and adapt as the economic environment impacts on our business, we no longer become a victim of chance.

When we step up and up-skill ourselves as the leader of our salon, spending more time as salon manager and salon CEO, we will no longer have to ask ourselves whether we will survive.

Because we know we can.

And not just survive…

…but thrive.

PART THREE

The Road to Recovery

CHAPTER 16 - FINDING WORKABLE SOLUTIONS.

As we've moved through this book, you will hopefully have realised that you are the key to getting your salon thriving again.

You are capable, but you need to nurture your resilience mindset and you need to be willing to take action to make this happen.

You will also have some understanding about how COVID has impacted your market, your clients, your staff and your role within the salon.

You will now know some of the problems you now face with COVID, as well as some of the opportunities that have revealed themselves.

Now is the time to look at solutions to the real-life problems that come with these pivot points in your ownership journey.

This section focuses on creating solutions to three common problems all salon owners face.

1. Managing quiet or slow periods
2. Successfully selling without feeling pushy or "salesy"
3. Stopping stress and uncertainty breaking down the salon culture *(this one is more dangerous to your business than you imagine.)*

This section will provide you with heaps of actionable steps that you can take to overcome these slumps and get your salon back on track.

The focus of this section is to create actionable steps that create forward momentum that moves you closer to where you want to be.

QUIET OR SLOW PERIODS

CHAPTER 17 – THE ROOT OF THE PROBLEM

We've all been in that situation when we've looked at the booking system and see large tracts of white space staring back at us.

We're not alone in feeling the panic start to rise in the pit of our stomach.

Hearing our mind start to panic with fear-based talk.

All salon owners know that feeling of looking at the work ahead and wondering, when are the clients going to come?

Will I have enough income to cover costs?

Is this the beginning of the end?

When we notice quiet or slow periods, this is the best time to make sure we maximise the clients we DO have.

This is the best way to start working smarter and not harder.

Tapping into our salon's systems, and using them to keep track of our stylist's performance, is really key to making the most of the clients we do have.

When doing this, it's important to keep focus on the consultation process. Monitor the customer service Key Performance Standards and support stylists with training and incentives to move stylist's figures towards where you need them to be to ensure all clients are getting a strong consultation that identifies and solves genuine problems for them.

When a client feels like the stylist understands their personal hair struggles, they are more responsive to listening to and taking recommendations from stylists.

Stylists should be encouraged and coached to offer solutions to the problems the client discusses in the consultation.

It is important to view strong Key Performance Standard results as a measure of the solutions stylists offer, rather than their sales ability.

By working with our salon's systems to grow our stylists' Key Performance Standards, we are in fact developing the value for clients in their visit to our salon.

This value is the non-tangible part of the service that grows client loyalty, increases client spend and strengthens the salon brand.

Quiet times are an excellent opportunity for the salon staff to work on developing and perfecting client consultations so they are easy to deliver and continue to delight clients when things get busier again.

As part of the focus on Key Performance Standards that should be focused on during quiet times, there is one that we need to pay particular attention to if we want to reduce the risk of quiet times plaguing our salons in the future.

And this is Rebooking.

CHAPTER 18 – KEEP THEM COMING BACK

Rebooking is one of the hardest Key Performance Standards to master.

This can come as a surprise to many people in appointment-based industries because on the face of it, rebooking should be the easiest of tasks because you are not actually asking for any more money.

But what we fail to recognise is that we are actually asking for two things that can be far more valuable than money …

> … time and trust.

When we ask a client to rebook, we are in effect, asking them to guarantee spending more time with us and that they trust us to give them what they want in the future.

This can be a hard thing to ask of clients.

And a hard thing for clients to commit to.

A stylist's rebooking figures can tell us a lot about their skill as a commercial stylist.

I have included a table in the back of this book that gives you a brief overview of what a stylist's rebooking rates can tell us about their confidence and skill.

To grow your salon's rebooking rates, there are two things that MUST happen:

1. Rebooking must become part of the consultation.
2. Training needs to support rebooking growth

And this won't be news to many.

"*Rebook in the chair*" has been a mantra of the industry for a while.

And training is the key to seeing any sizable growth in the business.

But there are good reasons to focus our energy on developing our salon's rebooking rates.

Rebooking is the number one way to create future work for the salon.

It means that we need to rely less on walk-ins and clients self-referring.

On slow days, it is much easier to fill empty space if it's only 20% of the salon's time rather than 60%.

It also gives us confidence about staffing rates and the ability to pay wages and bills when we have a handle on how much work we have ahead of us.

Rebooking also means we have permission to contact these clients directly should we need to.

If a stylist calls in sick or the salon needs to make a change to the client's appointment to better manage workflow, it is easier to do this if you have a client booked in.

When we neglect rebooking, we are at the mercy of a fickle market, never knowing whether we will have enough staff or clients to meet demand.

Rebooking also allows us the opportunity to collect important contact information. This is where the real value in our client list exists.

Having clients that have been to our salon is not helpful unless you can contact them again and add them to mailing lists.

Rebooking also works to support the salon brand as it is a great way to show clients that we value their time and their schedules by creating space in our future that is reserved just for them.

But what happens if we don't have the clients booked in and we need to fill days quickly?

CHAPTER 19 – START TALKING AGAIN

The next thing to work on is contacting those clients who have been to us before.

Think about sending out an email or text message announcement letting old clients know that spaces are available, or you have a product on promotion they might be interested in.

This is a great time to let them in on what they have been missing out on.

Share evidence of the work the salon is producing.

And tell them about the new COVID Health & Safety processes that have put in place to ensure they are protected while they are in the salon.

We never know why clients haven't come back, and sometimes all they need is a gentle reminder that we are still there.

And text message and email communication is not just for non-returning clients.

Contacting clients before their appointment to confirm a booking decreases the chances of no-shows and last-minute cancellations.

Our clients want to show up for us so it is important we support them to do this.

Reminding clients about up-and-coming appointments is not the only benefit of contacting our clients.

These are opportunities to share new products, services and promotions with existing clients which helps them feel connected to us between visits and excited about coming back to see us.

When clients feel excited about coming, rather than just something on their to-do-list, they are more likely to keep their appointment, and treat themselves to add-on services and products.

The most obvious place to let clients know about available appointments, and find new clients to join our salon's family is through Social Media posts and ads.

Clients love seeing us pop up on their news feeds. They especially love seeing our work and hearing from the team and their stylist, so make sure you involve the whole team when it comes to creating content.

Alongside keeping current clients up-to-date with salon happenings, social media is a powerful way to warm up a cold audience and introduce them to our salon.

Unfortunately, social media has the lowest return for the investment in time and money when it comes to finding new clients, but we definitely can use it to enhance brand status, brand awareness and increase engagement with your brand.

CHAPTER 20 – INVITE THE BEST

If you are looking for a more successful way to grow your client list with more of the clients that pay well and ask for services that you love doing, there is a simple, but underutilised, trick …

… ask your best clients to bring their friends.

Creating a referral scheme in your salon is a great way to encourage your best clients to bring in more clients like them.

A well-structured referral systems works on a number of levels.

It allows you to identify your best clients and let them know they are who you would like more of in your salon.

Personal recommendations are the BEST way to get more clients quickly so you get a great return on the investment.

Good referral systems create an opportunity to show those clients who support you by bringing their friends and family to you that you appreciate their commitment and loyalty to you and you are showing this with amazing rewards that are only offered to the best clients.

But these systems can take some time to bed down.

So what if we're having a quiet day today, what else can we do to stop the time being wasted?

CHAPTER 21 – SHOW THEM THE WAY

The best way to use unexpected downtime is with training.

Staff training is critical for any successful business.

Ultimately it is what makes our job, as the business owner, easier in the long run.

Training develops the quality of client appointments by growing outcomes and supports the business brand by ensuring there is consistency between each client visit and each stylist working within our salon.

But knowing what topic to train can be a minefield ...

... and a daunting idea.

In looking for an easy place to start, head over to your Stylist Performance Plan *(if you don't know what this is, I have a description in Appendix 2 at the back of this book).*

This is a great place to know which area in your salons need work, where stylists need development and how to create more understanding, and therefore better results, on current promotions or focus areas within the salon.

If we are thinking about trying some training during down time, there are three broad areas that we can draw ideas from.

The first is obvious, and necessary, hairdressing skills. These are the practical skills stylists need to perform their job.

And even if we're not comfortable teaching stylists new skills, going back over basics is a great way to support teamwork and reduce avoidable errors.

The second area that we can spend unexpected downtime training is on salon processes.

The how our salon does things.

This is a really good option especially if the downtime is staggered between stylists.

You can easily train salon processes one-on-one or in small groups.

In fact small group or one-on-one training is often MORE effective when it comes to making these processes stick.

This is the time for us to make sure our staff are running the salon to our standards, and it gives them opportunities to ask questions ...

... and give feedback and ideas for our consideration for future development of our salon systems.

Finally, the third thing we can train our stylists on ...

... and this is the IMPORTANT one ...

.. if you really want to shift the needle in your business when it comes to making more money from less clients then you need to be training your stylists in ...

            ... developing their consultation skills.

Growing our stylist's consultation skills is the #1 way to grow the value of each client AND keep clients coming back.

And there is a number of ways we can train this.

We can do it by Key Performance Standard, Client Demand Profile or Process.

They all work.

They're all important.

And you cannot EVER train consultation enough in your salon.

Using the Stylist Management Plan will allow you to know where consultation training needs to be focused and allow you to track the results.

CHAPTER 22 – MOVE THE TEAM FORWARD

To support training, another thing that can be done during down time is one-on-one meetings with your team.

Although these should ideally be scheduled in at regular intervals throughout the year, stylist one-on-ones are something that is commonly missed out on when owners are busy in their salons.

But when there are gaps appearing in your booking system, grab some time to get together with each of your stylists to talk about how they are going.

One of the most common reasons I hear from owners as to why they are not doing stylist one-on-ones more regularly is …

… that they are unsure about what to talk about to motivate stylists to perform better.

So I'm going to let you in on a trick.

There are only two things that you really need to talk about with your stylists during one-on-ones if you want to grow their productivity.

The first one will feel kind of obvious.

And this is the stylist's current performance.

This includes all the usual things like where they current performance is compared to expected results, performance goals and how they are performing against any specific productivity focus the salon has been working on recently.

The second thing to work on is goal setting.

This might not seem as important, but it is motivating for stylists to know how their time working for us is going to grow them and their careers.

When it comes to goal setting, it's important to link back personal and professional goals to the salon's Stylist Management Plan.

This is because as stylists work towards their goals they should be also hitting salon Key Performance Standards and Training Standards.

This will allow them to move along the Stylist Career Pathway and through the salon pricing structure.

Which will in turn allow them to access better employee benefits and new commission systems and bonus schedules which will support them to reach their goals, while powerfully moving the salon towards our goals.

CHAPTER 23 – GET YOUR HOUSE IN ORDER

And if you just have a little bit of down time or a sudden cancellation ...

... then just jump in and ask stylists who are not busy to start cleaning and organising the salon.

As a salon owner you will know that there is ALWAYS cleaning and organising to do.

And many hands make light work.

Down time is a fantastic opportunity to give both the inside and the outside of the salon a deep clean.

This is the time to get to all those cleaning and clean-out jobs that you don't normally have time to do.

Take the time to look at your salon through the eyes of the client.
> What will they see when they walk up to the shop?
> What will reception look like from their perspective?
> What can they see when they are sitting in the chair?

These are important things to consider when we have the time to do so.

Although we keep the salon in top shape from our perspective as stylists and workers in the salon, taking the time to view things from the client's perspective ensures nothing is overlooked and our clients continue to be delighted every time they walk in the salon.

When things start picking up again, you'll be grateful for the time to get things sorted and cleaned.

Another area that is really important and NEEDS a quiet time to get done properly is stocktaking.

Stocktaking is an important part of effective salon management and something that needs to be done at least once a year.

But the more often you can do it, the more effective it is.

We have a lot of money tied up in our stock. It is a sizable asset that is easy to overlook when we are seeing it day in and day out.

Knowing your actual stock holding helps you save money in a number of ways.

Firstly, it allows you to list and collate all the stock you do have.

It can be amazing to realize what is actually sitting around the salon waiting to get out onto the shelves, and stocktaking is a great way to bring it all into focus.

Giving us an opportunity to clear out old, out-of-date stock and restocking the shelves with items that might have been hidden away.

The next is that you can put an accurate value on the stock you have in your salon when you take the time to count it all up.

This means that you have valuable information you can give to your accountant and insurance broker to make sure you are properly protected AND you are also getting the full financial benefit of carrying all that stock.

And finally, it allows you to make strategic decisions about what stock to continue to carry and what lines to let go of.

When we buy opening packs from a product company, they often include some of EVERYTHING in that range.

But the reality for us is that our salon may not need or indeed have demand for every item in that opening pack.

Stocktaking allows us to talk to our product company Rep with more confidence and knowledge about what works and doesn't work in our salon.

**HOW TO SUCESSFULLY SELL TO CLIENTS DURING
DIFFICULT TIMES**

CHAPTER 24 – GETTING BACK TO BASICS

When times get tough the first thing to go is our confidence in the economy. Put more simply, it is our confidence in the supply or availability of money.

We notice things are getting a bit harder. We're getting a bit quieter. Clients are expressing THEIR concerns about their income, job security or the state of the economy.

This is a combination that is sure to have us heading on a fast track towards a feeling of lack.

And that is a dangerous place to find ourselves as the business owner.

When we sit in a lack mindset, we start focusing on everything that is not going right. Everything that is not going the way we want it to.

And many of these things are outside of our control.

When we take too much time to focus on what's not working in our life we create a mindset that draws on fear, panic and worry.

We start working to protect and hold onto what we have, rather than focusing on where we are going and all the opportunities that the COVID crisis has opened up to us (Remember Part 1).

"But really I'm scared of losing everything I've worked towards", I hear you say. *"I'm comfortable with what I know and the future feels scary."*

If you can relate to these intrusive thoughts, then you're not alone.

In times of crisis this can become the main track playing in the heads of all business owners.

But this doesn't serve you well. It affects your energy you put out. It will create a grasping and desperate energy that flows down to your staff, your clients and into your money.

What you spend your time focusing on, is what you end up getting. Focusing on losing money will make this happen to you.

On the other hand, focusing on nurturing the flow of positivity into your salon will make positivity flow to you.

It will create an authentic energy that is grateful and abundant that flows down to your staff, your clients and into your money.
Life doesn't happen TO us, it happens FOR us.

These crises and challenges in our journey are not signals that we are at the end, they are just re-directions back onto the better route for us, even if we can't see that right now.

Focusing on the right things in a positive and energetically aligned way (Remember Part 2) is the best foundation you can create to have your salon selling even when others aren't.

So where to begin focusing?

Over the next few chapters we will look at what you can do in your business right now so you and your team can sell authentically and keep clients excited about buying.

CHAPTER 25 - KEEPING IT CONSISTENT

When it comes to creating a space that clients feel safe to spend their money in, consistency is the key.

But don't think for a second this is me saying keep things the same as they were.

No. If you were right to keep things as they were then things would be fine and you wouldn't be here reading this book right now.
What I mean by consistency is get the basics right, then keep things moving forward in a planned and sustainable pace.

Clients get excited and enthusiastic when they are delivered a fantastic service. If they come back in again and the service is the same or better, then their confidence and trust in your salon grows.

If the service is weaker than they received last time, if the stylist seems to care less, offers less or consults less, then it reduces their confidence and trust in your salon and they are more likely to spend less.

As a good rule of thumb, the more a client trusts what is being delivered, them more likely they are to spend.

And the reverse is true too.

So how can we create consistency to grow trust between each client visit and between each stylist in the salon?

The number 1 way to do this is to train, train, train.

And when it comes to what to train, the answer may surprise you.

Although growing technical skills, like hairdressing skills, may seem like the obvious place to spend time training. When it comes to helping clients feel comfortable to spend it can have limited value.

The real powerhouse area to train is part of the service that is often overlooked for the more glamorous and alluring technical development training. And this is the consultation.

The biggest single part of the service that grows client spend, loyalty and your bottom line is the consultation.

The amount of importance that we, as the owners, place on the quality of ALL consultations conducted in our salon is the single biggest factor in determining how much money we make.

If you think spending time at every appointment doing consultations is not what your market wants, then you may as well give up now.

Time for a home truth …

In my experience, it is not the market that doesn't want to be consulted with and listened to at every appointment, it is just a story that stylists, and sometimes their bosses, tell themselves because they just do not know what to say to make consultation effective and not sound salesy.

If you are guilty of phoning-in your consultations from time to time, consider this:

If clients didn't care about appropriate questions being asked with a genuine focus on their hair, then the internet would not be filled with influencers, bloggers, vloggers and products that offer tips, tricks and solutions to personalise products and services to individuals.

When it comes to turning your business around, you need to get focused on consultations.

And this is where your training should start.

Training consultations can feel overwhelming because this is an area that WE may not have been properly trained in ourselves.

If this is the case, teaching others to do something we are not overly confident with can feel daunting.

But there are some steps you can take to make this process easier.

The first step should be to jump into your Stylist Performance Plan. (Check out Appendix 2 if you are looking to see what this is)

The three things you want to focus on here are the Customer Service Key Performance Standards, the current skill level of the stylists on your salon's Stylist Career Pathway and your salon's pricing structure.

As a stylist develops in their consultation skills they move through 3 broad stages in the consultation pathway. Each becoming progressively harder to master.

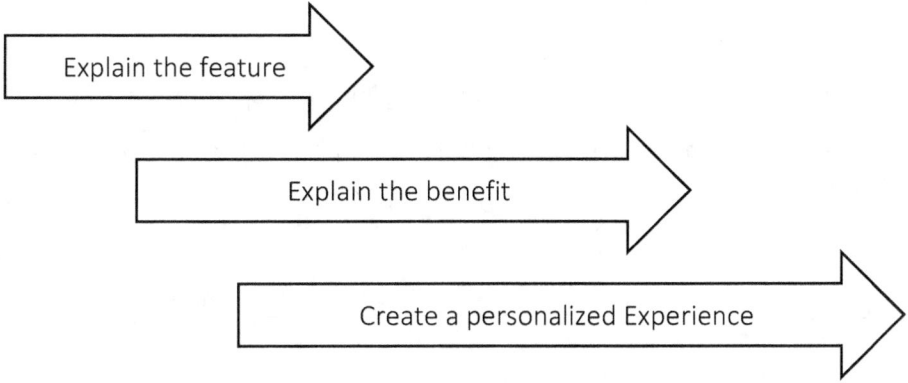

The first step is learning to **explain the features** of the product or service.

Broadly, this involves knowing the Manufacturer's Instructions and what the product does or the expected outcome of the service.

For example:

This shampoo that has ingredient (X) which will help protect your colour.

Or

By putting in foils through the top, we will make your colour appear lighter.

As a stylist develops in their skill, they begin to take those features and start to use them to **explain the benefit** for the client of having the service or using the product.

For example:
This shampoo will stop your colour fading between appointments by protecting it when you wash it. It uses this ingredient (X) as a key part of its technology to prevent early colour fade.

OR

To help blend your regrowth we can put some foils in through the top, we will make your colour appear lighter and mean that your regrowth will be less obvious between visits.

And as they become more experienced, they then move on to **making the recommendation more personal and emotionally connected with the**

client. Although this step is easy to do on paper, in reality it takes training and practice to get it right every time.

For example:
You were telling me about how you've been finding that your colour has been fading between visits. It's important that we keep this colour looking it's best for as long as possible because you said you loved how it really brings out your eyes because your boyfriend always comments on them, which you love.

By analysing your home haircare routine I have identified that there is something simple we can add to your routine to really make a difference in cutting down on colour fade. My recommendation is that you start including this shampoo into your home hair care routine as it is a proven way to stop your colour fading between appointments by protecting it when you wash it.

It uses this ingredient (X) as a key part of its technology to prevent early colour fade ensuring that every time your boyfriend, Jack, looks at you, your colour keeps your eyes the standout feature.

OR

We've been taking today a lot about how quickly you are finding your regrowth is coming through between visits and how it's making you more conscious of the amount of grey through the front.

That is totally understandable. We have our hair coloured to keep us feeling younger and our colour should work harder to make that happen for as long as possible. You've also said that you've been this colour for a long time and are feeling unsure about taking a dramatic change right now. This is normal.

As we discover an increase in grey through our natural colour, it is usual to have to adjust our colour to ensure it keeps us looking younger for longer. Today my recommendation to help blend your regrowth for longer is that we put some gentle highlights in through the top. Doing this we will make your colour appear slightly lighter, meaning that your regrowth will be less obvious between visits.

By just targeting the top today it will give as a seamless blend into your existing colour and a low commitment way to see how you like the changes. When you come in next time we can talk about how you found the colour and you can let me know your feeling on the change.

As you can see here, there is a definite progression from the entry point through to mastery.

And stylists may feel more confident moving up the consultation pathway in one area, like colours, and find it harder with others, like treatments or retail.

That is usual, and exactly why we as owners need to set standards, monitor and train all areas of the consultation for all stylists.

It is important that customer service Key Performance Standards are in step and align with your salon's Purpose and Unique Selling Point.

They should also be tiered to reflect the level of the stylist on your Stylists Career Pathway.

Doing these two things is important for keeping the standards high and encouraging stylists to engage authentically with their clients.

Add into the mix, a tiered pricing structure, and this becomes a really clear way to communicate between clients and stylists any changes in service between visits in a consistent way.

A tiered pricing structure means that all stylists that can perform services and deliver the consultation to the same level charge the same price.

The better they get, the more they charge.

This acts a reward for stylist who grow their hairdressing AND consultation skills, and as a clear guide to clients on the standard of service they can expect.

Training your staff is the only way to ensure consistency of service between stylists and across your team.

It is the only way to define minimum standards and grow service delivery for clients in a planned and sustainable pace.

A pace that grows clients confidence and desire to spend, rather than concerns them that everything is changing too quickly and they don't know what you stand for anymore.

CHAPTER 26 - LET THEM KNOW THEY ARE IMPORTANT

Training alone will not make sales feel authentic and effortless, planning is also required.

Planning is important because it allows us to demonstrate to every client at every appointment that they are important, and so is their time.

The key is approaching every appointment as if it is the most important appointment of the day.

And although planning is an obvious activity for us as salon owners, it is also something that your salon systems and processes should support stylists to do as well.

There is a number of ways you can incorporate planning and preparation into your salon's procedures.

The first is conducting mindset and attitude training.

This sound complicated but it is simply helping shift any assumptions stylists hold about which of their clients can afford to buy and how much they are prepared to spend.

When stylists hold on to these beliefs they limit themselves in their ability to deliver a top service and consultation to every client.

Having these assumptions makes stylists feel silly because they think they know what the client is thinking about them and their recommendations.

But the truth is they don't know.

And many of these assumptions are created from the stylist's own world view and personal insecurities.

By not training stylists to let go of these and view each client authentically, you are really limiting the success of your business to the level of your stylists' insecurities.

This is a dangerous place to be.

Mindset or attitude training should be scheduled regularly and could even be as simple as asking each team member during a team meeting to describe one thing that surprised them about their client when they offered something new.

Talking about these assumptions is the best way to bring them to the surface and remove them from your salon.

The next way to support your stylists to treat every appointment as the most important is to encourage them to keep detailed client notes and records.

Although many stylists keep records of the colour services they perform, very few keep records of what was talked about, important things going on in their client's life, future plans for their hair, any ongoing concerns and what was recommended even if it wasn't purchased.

Keeping records to this degree might feel like extra work (which it is) but there are good reasons to make the effort.

Detailed notes make it SO much easier to make every client feel special, even when you are busy.

It allows stylists to pick up the conversation exactly where it was left off. Helping clients instantly feel like part of the team.

It allows them to recommend products and services consistently and provide a clear reason if the recommendation changes because they have notes on what was recommended and why.

It allows stylists to develop a future plan for services which makes clients excited about coming back, and therefore more likely to rebook AND keep their appointment.

It also helps keeps stylist stress levels down.

Humans are hard wired to be social creatures. Research has shown us that we have an amazing capacity to hold detailed and complex information about the lives of others in our head.

We thrive and feel connected with those around us when do this. So it's in our nature to ask intimate questions, share and bond with other people.

But, like everything, there is a tipping point and something that brings us so much pleasure can start to cause us pain if we get too much of it.

The ideal number of connections we can hold in our head is between 50 and 150. It varies from person to person but most people are up around the 150 mark.

Once we get over our limit, we start to feel stressed and need more time to unwind, isolating ourselves from others.

The average stylist does about 25 clients a week and has an average cycle of 6 weeks. This means that the average stylist has about 150 clients that they see regularly.

150 clients leaves very limited space for family and friends.

Without writing down detailed client notes and releasing the information from their minds, stylists either start to think of the clients as their friends or they start to struggle with stress.

Neither of these two things support professional excellence.

Although holding client information in their head is not the only stress stylists will experience in their life, it is one that can be managed and removed.

Having detailed client notes also helps stylists prepare for the day ahead.

Stylists should be taught to plan for each appointment at the start of the day.

Planning should include things like managing previous objections, knowing previous recommendations, knowing if future appointments are already booked, knowing what the client's plans are for their hair and planning who will assist them if required.

Having this information and being able to share it with the team as required is all key to making each appointment feel like it is the most important one of the day.

When clients feel that planning and focus on them, it drives loyalty and trust, which in turn naturally grows sales.

CHAPTER 27 - LET THEM KNOW YOU CARE

With consultation training in place to create consistent customers service between appointments and across the team, planning to make each appointment feel special, the next step is creating authentic conversations that grow sales effortlessly.

The method to do this is a simple concept, but one much harder to carry out.

It is: solve their problems for them.

Basically, this mean focus on their hair needs and find genuine solutions to them.

Although this sounds so obvious when I say it, it is something that takes training and practice to achieve successfully.

Discovering the real problems clients may have with their hair is not always a straight-forward path.

I once had a new client that came in to see me wanting a full head of foils.

She was very specific about how I should and shouldn't foil her hair. (We've all had those clients)

She knew a lot about what she wanted and was very insistent on having her hair done her way. But one thing she said made me wonder about her choices.

She insisted that I was not to use a toner. This seemed like an interesting thing to not want so I decided to dig a little further and understand why this was.

And the answer surprised me.

When I investigated the 'no toner' policy, she said it was because she liked how her hair sat with just the bleach and the toner made it too soft.

She admitted that she preferred the colour with a toner but the lack of volume bothered her more.

So, I asked her if getting enough volume in her hair was something that was important to her. It was like a revelation for her.

Finally, she had been given an opportunity to talk about the thing that was REALLY bothering her about her hair.

A long time ago this client had been given foils by a hairdresser and it had increased the porosity of her hair to the point where she was finally achieving the level of volume she had always wanted. Since then, she had become fixated that raw foils were the only thing to give her what she wanted.

Because, until she sat in my chair, they were the only thing offered to solve her problem.

But what she actually wanted was not raw foils, it was volume.
A lack of volume was her most pressing hair concern.

The reason she had become so demanding with her colour was that if it wasn't done exactly as she described, there would not be enough volume for her liking.

Every hairdresser she had seen until me had assumed that this client knew exactly what she wanted, and that was to have her foils done in a specific way.

They were right about her knowing what she wanted, but the assumption that it was the colour. These assumptions led to a string of new hairdressers for this client because without more detailed consultations these hairdressers couldn't ever deliver to her what she really wanted solved by them.

We talked about how to fix her volume issues.

Then we talked about the colour she actually wanted.

In the end, she walked out with both the volume and colour she wanted. She left my salon with a booking for 5 weeks and a bag full of products that were the real solutions to her most pressing problem – volume.

Conduct your consultations without expectations.

The biggest mistake hairdressers make is asking questions of the client that confirms the hairdresser's assumptions about what the client wants rather than questions that reveal the true nature of the client's relationship with their hair.

The following are some examples of questions that provide the client with the opportunity to reveal something that is not obvious from the service they are booked in for:

1. If you could change one thing about your hair, what would it be?
2. What is the one thing it is most important I get right today?
3. What frustrates you the most about your hair?
4. If you could steal a celebrity's hair, who would that be?
5. What is your biggest concern with your hair right now?

When you can identify and solve a client's most pressing hair concern it elevates you in their eyes as a professional.

When clients view you as a professional, they are more likely to take your recommendations on services, products to take home and when you need to see them again.

Asking appropriate and powerful questions is not something that will happen first try.

As the owner, there are some things you can do to encourage active listening from your stylist.

The first is train the active listening process.

If having more detailed consultations is going to be a new thing for your salon, encourage stylists to listen out for great questions being asked by other team members, and then copy them until they start to have the confidence to try their own questions.

You can keep team active listening training focused by role playing and using the more experienced members of the team to show by example what works for them.

This is a time to work together to find solutions and examples of questions that work for your market.

This will be something that needs ongoing training.

It is really difficult to get too good at asking appropriate questions so never feel like you've done too much training on this.

If your stylists are already doing it well, regular training will help keep active listening a focus of the salon, and will provide important learning for the more junior stylists.

In my experience, salons that can get the junior team to be good at active listening and asking appropriate questions make their junior stylists profitable quicker than by focusing only on hairdressing skills training.

And when we are working with junior stylists or stylists that are new to your salon, it is important to be mindful of their skill level around consultation.

This mean they may need more feedback, support and training to start achieving the results of the more Senior and Advanced stylists.

Patience and consistency are important. It may feel like it is taking ages for the stylists to develop a consultation that finds genuine concerns, but by keeping active listening and appropriate questioning at the forefront of our consultation delivery will allow sales to come authentically without feeling sleezy and pushy.

CHAPTER 28 - KEEPING IT REAL

Once stylists can identify a client's most pressing concern, it is important that the solutions are kept real.

What do I mean by this?

It means making sure that a client's expectations are managed appropriately.

This simply means being honest about results and potential outcomes.

It is a call to stylists to be brave and demonstrate their professionalism. Long term this will pay off far more than trying to get a sale over the line with bold promises or misleading claims.

It's the old adage, under promise over deliver.

Be honest and open about the timeframe, cost and typical outcomes when it comes to creating hairdressing results.

Stylists need to be encouraged to discuss with clients honestly about the level of commitment new hairstyles or colours will require to upkeep. Not being told this information BEFORE the hairdresser started the work is the number one pain point for clients when they get a new do.

Being honest about the time, money and commitment to create a look will often spark a conversation about more practical alternatives that will give the client the general "look" without things spiralling and becoming unmanageable for them.

It is the same for recommending products. Clients shouldn't be walking out believing one wash with their new shampoo and their hair will be repaired.

It's important that they understand that things may even feel worse before they get better. That most products take time and consistency to get results.

Managing expectations will help build trust and keep clients coming back for the professional advice and service.

As part of managing client expectations, it is important for stylists to think about how the hair style and / or colour will work to complement and enhance the client's natural beauty.

I have never had a client sit down in my chair and say to me, "I'm feeling awful, please make sure I walk out of here looking worse than I came in".

It never, ever happens.

Clients come to us to look and feel better.

They want to feel something they are not feeling now. They want to feel younger, fresher, tidier, trendier, more beautiful.

This means taking a pragmatic approach to client requests and offering subtle changes that will work better with skin and eye colouring, face shape, age and lifestyle.

The more a stylist can do this, the more valuable they are to clients.

This is where tiered pricing can help clients understand the level of personalisation they will get in their consultation, and ultimately their service.

To support stylists to offer meaningful advice and realistic outcomes for their client, it is important that hair and scalp analysis skills (trichology) are developed in salon.

This is a common area for stylists to only have a basic working knowledge of.

The more they are able to more deeply understand the head in front of them, the less mistakes and the better the recommendations.

If this is an area you don't feel confident in teaching, most quality professional salon brands have a Technical Trainer (and sometimes even courses) who can offer support in developing hair and scalp analysis skills within your team.

Keeping sales up during the COVID crisis requires a more authentic and holistic approach.

It requires stylists to do what they most want to do, make clients feel good.

It starts by keeping things consistent with regular consultations at every appointment with every client.

Then it is enhanced by planning to allow clients to know that each appointment is important by keeping detailed notes for continuity and preparation.

Sales come much easier when we let clients know we care by finding solutions to their most pressing hair concerns through active listening and asking appropriate and probing questions.

And finally, trust and professionalism grow client spends by offering knowledgeable assessments of timeframes, costs, outcomes and upkeep, being able to offer personalised recommendations and conduct thorough hair and scalp analyses.

Growing sales when things seem desperate is about being able to give back more.

By being able to offer a more exceptional customer service adds value and grows client trust.

It provides opportunities for sales recommendations to be made naturally and appropriately, which enhances the likelihood of clients to uptake these recommendations.

Creating an authentic way to develop sales in theory is not hard.

What is hard is that it requires us as owners to start setting performance standards and training our stylists to deliver these standards to every client at every visit.

But the reward is worth the effort we put in.

Growing your client sales will be critical to creating financial strength during these uncertain times.

**HOW TO STOP A STRESSFUL FEW DAYS/WEEKS/MONTHS
CRIPPLING YOUR SALON CULTURE AND POSITIVITY**

As we learnt in Part 1, the COVID crisis can bring unpredictable changes to how your salon usually operates.

It will affect client buying behaviour and may cause longer than usual periods with low client numbers or poor sales.

If your salon came into the crisis with a lower rebooking rate and / or informal systems, you may find these quiet periods going on for longer than you are used to.

This can play havoc with our sanity.

As we learnt in Part 2, owners keeping positive is critical to the overall success of our business, especially at this time.

In Part 2 we discovered ways to build a more positive mindset that was focused on gratitude instead of lack.

We looked at how to build resilience within ourselves and keep positivity alive, even in trying times.

In this section of Part 3, we are going to look at some practical steps we can take as owners to stop the rot of a negative mindset setting in at our salon and driving sales and opportunities away.

CHAPTER 29 – KNOW THE REACH OF YOUR CONTROL

In the drive to keep yourself and your salon a positive and thriving space it is important to keep focused on what you can control.

This may seem obvious enough, but a lack of discipline in this area is a fast track to hopelessness.

Training the mind to know the difference between what we can control and what we can't is a key skill of all successful people.

When stress grows, our minds can feel bombarded with things to panic and worry about.

Being able to know which ones are important is a valuable tool for all business owners.

A simple way to find the difference is to write down once a day all the things that are worrying us.

Set an alarm on your phone and when that goes off get to writing down everything you can think of that is causing you worry.

Don't hold back here. Write everything. Let it flood out.

When you feel the list is complete, go back over it and read each item out loud one by one.

As you read out each item, decide if you have any control over changing it.

If you don't, cross it out.

If you do, get to writing a plan to solve this worry or anxiety point.

Then take the plans you have written and compile a to-do-list for today, and then for the rest of the week.

When you feel anxiety and worry creeping back in, remind yourself that if you couldn't control it you have crossed it out, and if you can you have a plan to solve it.

Then stick to your plans, staying focused on what you can solve.

Creating plan and getting your salon's paperwork in order is really important if you are in lockdown and can't get the salon open. Staying focused on a more positive future is the only way to grow hope.

Hope is the seed of success.

CHAPTER 30 - KEEP THE COMMUNICATION FLOWING

When things start getting stressful, it is human nature to start keeping our own company more. It's normal to start shutting down communication.

If we are feeling stressed, out of control or even guilty for feeling so vulnerable we can find our communication drops away.

This is a normal thing to happen.

We do this because we are not always exactly sure what is happening or what is going to happen. It is hard to communicate something that we are not sure about ourselves.

So, when we see that we're finding it hard to have conversations with our staff, to let them know our plans and strategy to get through, that is EXACTLY the time to book a team meeting.

Although the idea of talking to our staff when we ourselves are feeling at a loss can be a daunting prospect, it is the exact right time to do it.

When we least feel like communicating, this is the time to really start.

When you have these conversations with your staff, be honest with them about your concerns.

Talk to them about your plans and ask them for feedback.

You don't have to include their feedback into the final shape of the plans, but it will serve you on two levels.

First your team may be able to see something that is not obvious to you.

And secondly, including them in the discussion will help keep them calm and feeling more secure that there is a plan to keep their job viable.

The biggest reason staff will leave a job during a crisis like this, is because they feel their job is at risk because there is not plan or structure to keep the money coming in.

Staff will be aware when there is a problem, and involving them in the conversation will help keep them focused on what they can change, which is their client service and growing their revenue.

CHAPTER 31 - BECOME A CREATURE OF HABIT

The best way to settle nerves and give yourself the courage to take the action to keep your salon moving forward is to develop a strong routine.

This means scheduling out time to work on your business and not in it.

Although servicing clients will give you that instant feeling you are doing something productive to help your salon, longer term, spending too much time on the floor will leave you vulnerable.

It is important that you schedule time out of your column on a regular basis to work through your plans, monitor and report back to your stylists on their performance, and train and coach your team to deliver their customer service to your standards.

Working through your plans will give you more piece of mind, and really help move things forward.

The biggest challenge in doing this, is keeping on task.

Staying on task is something some people find easier than others.

If you are one of those that struggle with this, make sure you keep a diary or schedule planner.

You can do this manually on online. Both work just as well as each other.

It is also important that you turn off your phone and app notifications during these important work times. This is because when we are working on more challenging plans, it is easy to become distracted by the more pleasurable strolls through social media.

Personal discipline will help here and keeping to your routine will make this easier over time.

So will creating accountability. Finding someone to report your progress back to is really helpful in the early stages of creating a routine.

It can be anyone you trust. Your partner, parent, friend or even a business coach or accountant.

As your personal routine tightens up, you will find a need to tighten up your salon's routine.

Keeping rosters and work schedules as consistent as possible will help with scheduling team meetings and training.

It will give you the confidence to book out time with each of your team members to have one-on-one catch ups on a regular basis.

It will also help shape an awareness in your salon that professionalism is important when it comes to making money.

It is really difficult to be professional amongst chaos.

While things are up in the air and stress levels are at risk of rising, it's also important to stick with what you know when it comes to the products and services you offer.

Introducing new products and services because they offer the promise of new revenue streams is risking adding a new level of complexity when there doesn't need to be.

Although new products and services are important when it comes to keeping your salon modern and relevant, it is important to do this with some planning and strategy behind it.

It is important to ask yourself whenever you are looking to introduce a new product or service whether it helps support your salon's Unique Selling Point and Salon Purpose.

If it doesn't, then let it go.

If it does, then ask yourself is what I am already doing to support the Salon's Purpose and Unique Selling Point (USP) done to the highest standard and will this new product or service elevate what we are currently doing?

If you are unsure, think about introducing it at a later date once the salon's current delivery of the USP has been developed.

Introducing too much too quickly, and without purpose or strategy, will be costly and just add pressure in areas that will not give you the best return long-term.

Now is the time to focus on growing what your salon is good at and slowly introduce new items with strategy and a plan.

CHAPTER 32 - TRAIN LIKE YOUR LIFE DEPENDS ON IT

When things are slowing down and your team is finding itself with more time in its hands, this is the time to ramp up training.

Quiet times can be excellent opportunities to get all staff familiar and on track with your salon systems.

Salon systems include how things should be done in the salon from cleaning to client care.

It includes how to consult, how to recommend, and how to check out a client.

If you are feeling unsure where to start, start simple.

The more you do it, the more you will refine your process.

It is easy to get overwhelmed when you're trying to get everything perfect before you start. But it doesn't need to be perfect it just needs to be happening.

Create a list of areas you want to train your staff on. And when one, some or all of your staff them have quiet times, get busy training them.

Teach your team how to work together to delight clients and get sales across the line.

Train them on the importance of meeting sales targets and Performance Standards.

Let them know why it is important the salon makes money and how they benefit from this.

Start to view quiet times as guidance from the Universe that your systems and process need tightening up and you have been given the opportunity to do this.

If you want your salon to be successful, it's important to recognise that it is your team that will get you there.

And the team never rises to the pressure of the occasion, rather they will sink to the level of their training.

This means that when the going gets tough, it is the strength of our training that gets us through – not the desire to succeed.

CHAPTER 33 - BRING JOY

Training your team is important. But so is bedding the training into their everyday practice.

Providing focus and opportunity for stylists to use and think about the training is so important when it comes to making good habits stick.

And the best way to do this is to bring positivity and fun to the table.

When things are looking down, it is time to take positive and motivational steps to capture stylist's focus and hold it until the new behaviour becomes second nature.

One of the quickest and most enjoyable tools you have are productivity challenges and performance incentives.

These are challenges that you set for one, some or all of your staff to grow their performance and be rewarded for it.

Productivity challenges are usually the first place to start.

This is where you choose an area of the customer service that you have been training and set a target for number of times that training is successfully employed.

The classic one here is retail. A target number of retail units to be sold is set, and when that target number is reached the stylist wins a prize.

These are the best place to start because it is really clear what needs to happen to win the prize.

You can adjust the target level based on the stylist's level within the salon or you can stagger prizes so the more they sell the more they get.

This is a great way to keep stylists motivated and focused on the area of the service they have just received training on.

Performance incentives are more advanced challenges that are rewards usually linked to a stylist's Key Performance Standards.

These are designed to grow a stylist out of their comfort zone, stretching their current level of performance.

Again, stylists will need training to support this growth but they are a great way to grow stylists individually and work on their weaker areas.

Another useful way to encourage positivity and joy in the salon is to use stylist-client linked promotions.

This type of promotion is especially good at boosting rebooking.

As we have already discovered, rebooking is one of the hardest Performance Standards to master and a stylist-client promotion helps to make this easier by reducing objections from the client.

The way something like this might work is to run a hamper raffle that every client who rebooks can go into the draw to win.
You then also provide a prize that the stylists wins if it is their client that is drawn out.

This is a great way to encourage both stylists and clients to embrace your customer service standards.

Boosting moral and keeping stylists enthusiastic during quieter times can be hard. A good way to pump excitement into the day is to run promotions that support the services and products they like doing and are confident selling.

This type of promotion is a great way to keep clients excited about your core products and services, promoting your salon's Unique Selling Point and Salon Purpose.

These promotions also have the added benefit of growing stylist confidence with quick and easy wins.

Often when things are quiet it can be easy to expect clients are not interested in buying. Being able to get a few good sales across the line can quickly flip a stylist's mindset into a more abundant one.

Running promotions and incentives is not the only way to boost stylist positivity and enthusiasm.

When things have been quieter, it is a great time to sit down with stylists one-on-one and set goals.

Setting goals allows you to easily connect stylist performance in the salon to the real-world goals they hope to achieve.

Showing stylists how growing their revenue will grow their wages through the commission or bonus system is a powerful reminder that professionalism and working to standards has its rewards which they can benefit directly from.

Setting and working towards personal goals through growing their revenue is a powerful way for stylists to stay motivated.

If you have already set goals with your stylists, take the time over the quieter periods to remind stylists of their goals and ask them to reaffirm how much achieving them would mean to them.

This is also a great time to develop a plan with each stylist to map out how they will achieve their goals quickly.

Once you have your stylists working through the training to develop their customer service and salon processes, working on quick win challenges or growth focused incentives, you are running promotions that make it easy for stylists to grow their performance and you have set individual goals that will inspire stylists and plans to achieve them that will motivate, the next step is to catch staff winning every day.

This means handing out praise and acknowledgement, small spot prizes, sweeties or just a simple "thank you" when you capture stylists being positive, living the salon values and working hard to achieve their results.

This is something that needs to be done every day, and often more than once.

It is important that stylists are told when they are doing something right.

The only way to really effect long-term culture change is to let stylists know when they are behaving how you want them to.

Acknowledging the right behaviour is about rewarding effort over results.

This is different from challenges, incentives, bonuses and commission where only the results are rewarded.

Acknowledging and rewarding the right behaviours, the right attitude and the right effort is the single most powerful thing you can do to get your team on board with your vision for recovery.

It is so easy to tell staff when they get things wrong, but it is far more powerful to let them know when they get things right.

A quick strategy here is create yourself a high-five chart. (there is one in Appendix 3 for you to copy)

In the first column list all the stylist's names.

Then every time you consciously thank or reward stylists getting it right, put the date and keep filling it. Reward yourself if you complete the chart in a week.

Do this as many times as it takes to make winning and success a habit in your salon.

THE NEXT STEPS

The COVID-19 crisis is an awful thing to happen to a small business like yours.

Absolutely.

And it won't be the last crisis you or your business will face.

Having to navigate through the unexpected is the nature of being in business.

It is something EVERYONE in business faces at one time or another.

Sometimes it small and temporary such a pipe bursting or the EFTPOS machine breaking down.

Other times it could be closer to home and feel more life changing, such as an accident, a new baby, or a personal tragedy.

And sometimes it's just the movement of time that brings foreboding and unrest in the form of an economic change, a pandemic, war or political unrest.

These things happen to all businesses.

And business with shaky foundations will be the most at risk.

As we come to the conclusion of this book, you will be starting to see a theme emerging.

The theme is that it is never too late to start building solid foundations, start anywhere and train those foundations into your team.

Putting planned and organised structure into your business will make it easier to make money and grow your wealth.

More money and structure will create more stability, meaning you are able to pivot and recover faster when things go wrong.

Structure and stability will mean you can take more time off the floor, and give yourself the freedom small business ownership should provide.

Structure and more freedom will help you create a plan with purpose that helps support a more positive and future focused outlook when it comes to dealing with your staff.

Structure and a more positive outlook will create a staff culture that grows sales and keeps clients coming back.

Structure doesn't mean that you won't have to work hard, it means you know that your hard work is leading somewhere.

At the end of this book you will now be able to start identifying some of the opportunities that the COVID-19 crisis will offer you.

This book only really looks at these in broad strokes, but as you become more aware of the opportunities around you, you will notice specific opportunities that are there just for you and your business to grab hold of.

You will now understand that the survival of your business comes down to you and your mindset, resilience and determination to see the business through this.

It comes down to your preparedness to add more structure and rigor to how your business runs.

And you will be starting to see that the solution to almost all of the problems we face in our business is around improving engagement and trust of staff and clients though consistently applied salon plans and structures.

You are heading in the right direction if you are ready to take action and start the recovery process in your salon.

For resources featured in this book or further information relating to this book, visit www.profitablesaloncreator.com/cut_your_losses

RESOURCES

For printable versions of these resources go to
www.profitablesaloncreator.com/cut_your_losses

APPENDIX 1 – WHAT A STYLIST'S REBOOKING RATES TELL YOU ABOUT THEIR SKILL AS A COMMERCIAL STYLIST.

Rebooking Rate	Meaning	Consequence
< 10%	<ul><li>Stylist is not discussing rebooking.</li><li>Stylist cannot deliver the salon service as required.</li></ul>	<ul><li>Relying solely walk-ins to fill day.</li><li>Stylist has no clients of their own.</li><li>Never makes bonus.</li></ul>
11% to 35%	<ul><li>Often a Trainee.</li><li>Little or no rebooking training.</li><li>Inconsistent focus on rebooking.</li><li>Service is usually delivered inconsistently.</li></ul>	<ul><li>Relying heavily on walk-ins and has some clients.</li><li>Rarely make bonus.</li><li>Stylist has high client turnover.</li></ul>
36% to 55%	<ul><li>Stylist is not able to confidently understand client's needs.</li><li>Service is often delivered inconsistently.</li></ul>	<ul><li>About half the column is full.</li><li>Relying on walk-ins to achieve bonus.</li><li>Column not growing.</li></ul>
56% to 65%	<ul><li>Stylist is discussing rebooking regularly, but usually at front desk.</li><li>Service is starting to be delivered consistently</li></ul>	<ul><li>Stylist is starting to be busy, especially on some days.</li><li>They can make bonus.</li><li>Stylist is slowly growing their column but not actively.</li></ul>
66% to 75%	<ul><li>Stylist is sometimes discussing rebooking in the consultation.</li><li>Service delivery is often consistent.</li></ul>	<ul><li>Stylist is quite busy, especially on some days.</li><li>They are growing their column but not consistently.</li><li>They sometimes make bonus.</li><li>They are developing</li></ul>

		good relationships with the clients they feel comfortable with.
76% to 85%	• Stylist is often discussing rebooking in the consultation. • Stylist usually delivers service consistently.	• The stylist is usually busy most days. • They are able to manage their working week well. • Their column is growing. • They often make bonus. • They have good relationships with most clients.
86% to 95%	• Stylist is always discussing rebooking in the consultation but has some clients offering objections the stylist is struggling to overcome. • Able to always deliver the salon's service standard.	• This stylist is always busy. • They usually make bonus. • They have a good ability to manage their column to suit their needs. • They have strong relationships with most clients.
96% +	• Always discusses rebooking with every client, every time and often multiple appointments in advance. • Always delivers the salon service to the highest standard.	• This stylist is always busy • Always makes bonus. • Their column is highly managed and rarely have down time. • They have a highly professional relationship with every client. • Often have waiting list.

APPENDIX 2 – THE 7 PARTS OF AN EFFECTIVE STYLIST PERFORMANCE PLAN

1. **Stylist Career Pathway** – the backbone of the Stylist Performance Plan

This is the steps a stylist will take as they move through your salon, increasing in skill, experience and performance. These are organised tier or levels that have clear links to performance criteria, employee benefits, commission systems, bonus, charging-out rates and training expectations.

The stylist career pathway helps stylists know where they sit in the salon hierarchy, who is above them and who is below. It also helps them understand why they get what they do, and what they need to achieve to get more.

2. **Performance Standards** – The engine behind productivity

These are the customer service and financial targets stylists need to meet as they move through the salon.

By attaching them to the Stylist Career Pathway, stylists understand what the minimum standard is for their level, where they are currently performing and what they need to achieve to progress.

These standards allow you assess performance without being in the salon.

3. **Employee Benefits** – The Key to unlocking staff engagement

These are the non-cash benefits your staff get for working for you. It is usual for salon owners to give much of this away and not expect anything in return.

Not identifying everything owners give their stylists and not expecting standards to be met to get them is the biggest driver of resentment between owners and their staff.

4. **Stylist Training** – The fuel for growth

This is the training stylists receive, the cost of this and the training they deliver.

Having a training schedule allows you to keep track of skills development, quickly identify knowledge gaps and keep the team moving forward.

It is the key to sustainable salon growth and performance.

5. **Salon Pricing Structure** – The muscle behind profitability

A salon pricing structure is the best way to keep stylists motivated and clients excited about coming back.

A salon pricing structure rewards top performers, drives client loyalty to the salon and helps keep service delivery consistent across the salon.

6. **Commission systems** – The oil that keeps everything moving.

A good commission system requires planning to develop to ensure the right behaviours and results are rewarded.

It also needs to be structured to it is easy to explain and understand so stylists know exactly what they need to achieve every day to grow their revenue.

APPENDIX 3 – HIGH-FIVE CHART TEMPLATE

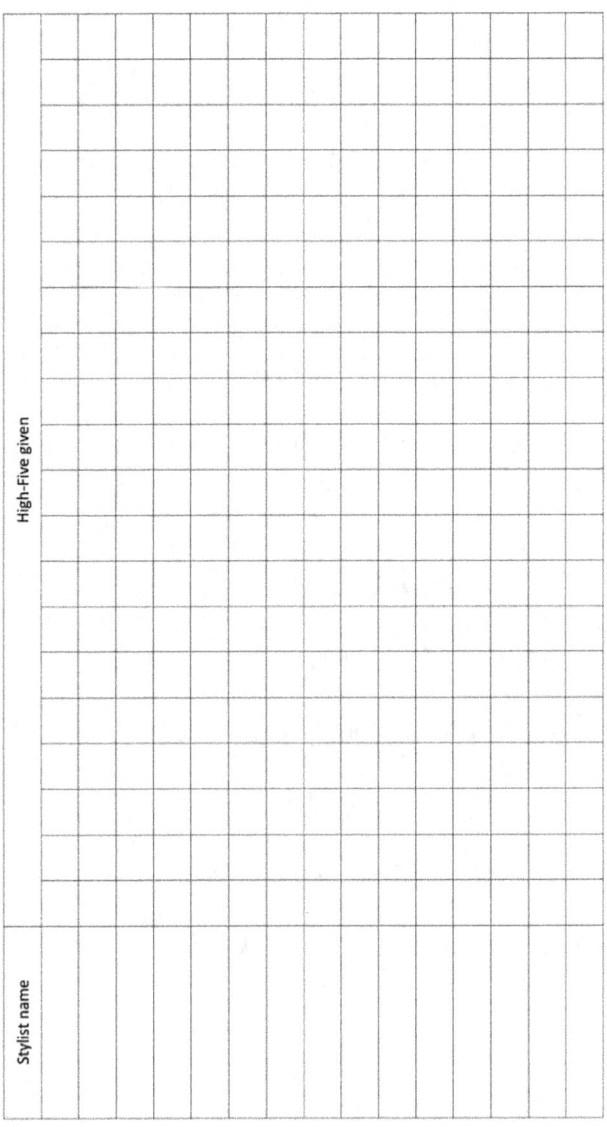

APPENDIX 4 – COPY OF MANTRAS FOR POSITVE SELF-BELIEF

Mantras for cultivating positive self-belief and leadership success:

I am worthy

I am doing the work needed

I am not alone

Others are excited by my success

I am working every day to get through this

I am investing in my personal growth

My personal growth is important

I am a strong leader in my salon

I ask for help when I need it

Success is on its way to me

My team is energised by my leadership

My salon thrives under my leadership

Abundance flows from the work I do as a leader

ABOUT THE AUTHOR

Hi, my name is Caroline Cooper and I'm a small-business systems specialist and productivity expert.

I founded Profitable Salon Creator, an online platform for salon and other appointment based business owners to grow their businesses and develop mastery of them.

Profitable Salon Creator was developed because I know the importance of supporting owners to effortlessly develop profitable systems and powerful structures.

These systems and structures are essential in allowing owners to quickly and knowledgably deal with their most pressing concerns, growing confidence and motivation to continue.

I have been in small business ownership for over 20 years, including over 10 years as a salon owner, and I am passionate about small business growth and profitability.

My passion has grown from my belief that small businesses are the backbone of the economy and need to be supported to provide sustainable and meaningful jobs within our communities.

I work most closely with salons because I know that thriving salons provide financial security and achievement to women in a female centric workplace.

Strong, profitable, female focused workplaces create sustainable, meaningful and engaging employment, uplifting all of the women in them.

www.ingramcontent.com/pod-product-compliance
Lightning Source LLC
Chambersburg PA
CBHW070637220526
45466CB00001B/211